JENNIPHER M. ZULU

THE WRITING
BUSINESS

"What Writers and Everyone Else Should Know"

A BOOK THAT WILL CHANGE YOUR
PERSPECTIVE ON WRITING

JENNIPHER M. ZULU

THE WRITING
BUSINESS

"What Writers and Everyone
Else Should Know"

A BOOK THAT WILL CHANGE YOUR
PESPECTIVE ON WRITING

A publication of Eagle Books

P.O. Box 50094, Lusaka

Copyright © 2024 by Jennipher .M. Zulu

All rights reserved. This book or any portion thereof may not be reproduced or used in any manner whatsoever without the express written permission of the publisher except for the use of brief quotations in a book review or scholarly journal.

First Printing: 2024 USA

ISBN: 9798328965873

Edited by: Juliana N. Mill
Proofread by: Anthony Onugba

JZ Books
P.O. Box 50094
Lusaka 10101

www.jzanessteps.weebly.com

Ordering Information;
Special discounts are available on quantity purchases by corporations, associations, educators, and others. For details, contact the publisher at the above-listed address.

Bookstores and wholesalers: Please contact Jennipher .M. Zulu
Tel: (+260) 979-888824; or email:
jennifer.zulu@yahoo.com

WHO IS THIS BOOK FOR?

Writing and selling books is a thriving industry with immense potential. This book encapsulates knowledge gained from years of experience in both writing and business. It is dedicated to writers, readers, and business-minded individuals seeking opportunities across various industries—those looking for innovative ideas and inspiration.

It is my earnest hope and sincere prayer that you find this book helpful and relevant, and that it encourages you to view writing from a business perspective, unlocking the many opportunities it offers.

PRAISE FOR WRITING AS A BUSINESS:

Sydney Muponda, PhD
Storyteller | Literary Expert

"Jennifer M Zulu's 'Writing as a Business' is a game-changing masterpiece that every writer, aspiring or established, needs to have in their arsenal. In this remarkable work, Jennifer lays out a tremendous account of how writing is not just a craft, but a thriving business and a vital component of the Creative Industries and Economy. With her deep insights and practical guidance, Jennifer empowers writers to view their passion through an entrepreneurial lens, equipping them with the tools and strategies to transform their creative talents into sustainable, profitable ventures. This book is a must-have, not just for its informative content, but for the way it ignites a sense of excitement and possibility for the future of the writing profession. 'Writing as a Business' is an important and thrilling book that will inspire you to approach your craft with a renewed sense of purpose and the confidence to claim your rightful place in the dynamic world of the Creative Economy. Jennifer's expertise and the sheer power of her words will leave an indelible

mark on your journey as a writer. This is a book you cannot afford to miss."

Mweeni Phiri
Author – Industry Expert

"This book introduces fundamental concepts that can transform the writing industry. While the writing industry has yet to reach its full potential, the future is bright.

This book is a toolkit for writers, offering processes and insights to elevate an author's career. By adopting these methods before publishing, authors can enhance their understanding of the industry and achieve greater success.

As authors aim to maximize book sales, this guide will keep them on track. It's a step in the right direction."

ACKNOWLEDGEMENTS:

First and foremost, I want to thank God for the gift of writing.

Secondly, I'd like to express my deepest gratitude to my friends and family for their unwavering support and encouragement, which has enabled me to put my thoughts and feelings into words.

Lastly, I want to thank everyone who will purchase this book. Your support fulfils my purpose and desire as a writer.

CONTENTS:

Who is this book for?	iii
Praise for 'Writing as a Business'	iv
How I got myself into writing	1
Why write?	4
Where to start from	10
Correcting the misconceptions	15
The fair and best way out	33
Writing as a business	35
Financial Management	57
Planning	60
Plan templates	65
The writing industry	77
Opportunities in the writing industry	86
What to write	82
Understanding publishing	84
Writing as a side-hustle	96
What to write	100
Copyrights	109
Government's role in the writing industry	112
Inspiration note	115

HOW I GOT MYSELF INTO WRITING:

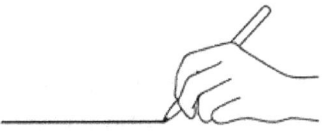

"The art of writing is the art of discovering what you believe." – **Gustave Flaubert**

In my first year of secondary school, my father sat me down in our living room to ask me what I wanted to study after completing grade twelve. I had been looking forward to that moment, and I could recall feeling all grown and mature when he asked me the question. I thought, *'This is it—it's time to answer the serious question of life.'* What did I want to do after school?

I clasped my hands and put on a formal attitude accompanied by a serious face as I prepared to respond. I gave my father three possibilities, and writing was not one of them. Even to me, writing was nowhere near my mind. I told him I wanted to study law, architecture, or medicine. The courses were not one bit related. They came to mind because I had the brains to take on any of them. At the time, I believed they were the ultimate careers one could opt for, and I guess so did my father.

I think he was pleased with my choices because he never disputed them, nor did he offer any other alternative. Instead, he delved right in to discuss the options I had put on the table. We chatted for a while, and when we both ran out of words to further our discussion, he encouraged me to study hard and assured me that I would make it. He then stood up and left for his room. He looked satisfied with the outcome of the discussion, and I sure was.

So, to further validate my thoughts of maturity and being grown at the time, I picked up a newspaper, which was my father's favorite pass-time tool when at home, and read almost all the published articles there, even though I could not make much sense of what had been written because it was technical jargon for my age. I was in grade eight. Newspapers were an 'adult' thing, in my point of view.

Fast forward to the future, I never became a lawyer, I never became an architect, and neither did I study medicine. Instead, I studied Business Administration and started a literary organization fifteen years after stumbling into writing while writing some good advice on life, which turned out to be 109 pages long.

After five years in the writing sector, I learned all I could learn and saw everything I needed to see. I saw the challenges, the opportunities, and the many existing gaps. The five years also bore a deep passion for seeing writing blossom and develop in my country; to see the creative writing sector established so it could yield its potential and get where it ought to be.

Along the way, I wanted to give up many times because it was not easy, but my passion had already grown its roots in me, and I just wanted to make a difference in any way I could.

This is the background of my writing life.

So, why write?

JENNIPHER M. ZULU
WHY WRITE?:

"To write is to discover." – **Frances Mayes**

When someone says they are looking for a job or looking to start a business, especially this side of the world, where not much investment has been made in the literary sectors or where the literary sectors are either underdeveloped or almost non-existent, one of the last options in mind is investing in anything writing-related. Well, the reasons are almost obvious. Anyone investing is looking for revenue or other significant returns, which is usually not the case because of the above reasons.

Many in these areas consider writing to be a hobby for people with nothing else to do, people with no employment opportunities, or people who cannot find anything else meaningful to keep them busy.

From an analytical or logical point of view, many say writing has very little value in monetary terms for anyone to take it seriously as a career. That said, there is almost no parent who would want to send their child to school so that they can become a writer after investing so much in their education.

Many of us who are writing just stumbled into the art while pursuing other paths in life. Even the idea of going to university to advance writing skills is usually daunting until a clear success path in the art is set. Many would rather learn and develop their writing skills through experience.

There has been a lot of debate, and arguments as to whether there is real value in one becoming a full-time writer. I would want to categorically say that yes, there is real value in writing as a full-time career even in areas where the literary sector is underdeveloped, and this is to answer the question 'why write?'

Many bestselling authors today are valued at millions of dollars, and all that is from book sales. Dr Seuss, a renowned children's book writer has sold well over 300 million book copies. J.K Rowling, the famous writer of the *Harry Potter* series is another renowned billionaire in the global writing industry. Africa boasts of the likes of

Chinua Achebe, Chimamanda Ngozi Adichie, Zukiswa Wanner, Ayobami Adebayo, Mohale Motsigo, and many others that are minting good money from proceeds of their book sales.

When the writing industry is well established, it can earn millions of dollars in revenue from book sales and writing-related services, which include editing, formatting, consultancy, ghost writing, and book and e-book publishing. The industry also draws in forex for its exported products, making it very lucrative. Furthermore, the industry creates employment and opportunities for a varying range of professions through publishing houses and agencies offering writing-related services. The professions include marketers, distributors, lawyers, accountants, graphic designers, etc. This makes the industry relevant as it contributes not only to the country's GDP and the global GDP, but also to the United Nation's development goals.

When the industry is not established, a writer can target to write for the world. Writing provides tremendous opportunities in this regard because consumers of the art come from everywhere around the world. A writer's works can travel to far-flung places that, in many cases, the writer themselves may never travel to.

The greater reward of writing is often seen to be a game of luck, or competition for better writing talent, and the like. However, in as much as some people are well endowed with an almost natural command of writing skills, writing can be learned and mastered. Of course, some would say they were born with it or born for it but anyone can learn writing at almost any stage of their life. Suffice it to say, however, that like everything else, one tends to perform better when they start developing their skill, or talent early in life to master it, although I believe that one can still learn, catch up, and even surpass those who started earlier.

Many writers that I have come across, and those I know from reading about them, or watching documentaries about them, initially go into writing because they discovered a passion for the art, or they learned that they actually have a talent in writing. These write for the love of the art and the fulfilment it brings them; the inexpressible excitement of finishing a manuscript, seeing their name printed on the book, and watching people purchase the book. I can equally attest that it's an invaluable feeling of achievement.

Sometimes, writers write to pour out their bottled emotions, to express themselves, to voice out, and better still, to heal. Most writers are guilty of putting outlines of their own experiences in the pieces they write. Some have gone on to detail things they would never tell the world but expressed them as scenes, stories, or advice to the reader. I'm guilty too. We have different ways in which we express ourselves and bring out issues, especially those closest to our hearts. Others talk to people about their issues, some sing about them, while some of us write.

Writing is equally a source of healing, comfort, and closure for readers as well. Many people just want someone to tell them that they are doing fine, that it's ok. They want other people's stories that they can relate to. These stories are written in books by a writer. Through this, the writer becomes very important and necessary in the circle of healing. So as writers, many times, if not all the time, we write for others as a way of reaching out, and as a way of holding someone else's hand. We write for healing.

Others get into writing for the business opportunities they identify in writing. Just like the theme of this book, writing is a business to them. Writing sometimes is a facet of a business venture. Talk of motivational speakers and church leaders, for whom it is also a ministry. Talk of politicians, and other influential figures. Writing for them brings in supplemental income.

Many other reasons can be cited as to why one can take up writing and we may not be able to delve into all of them here. Let's just say, hell yes! Or perhaps, heaven yes! Writing presents many great opportunities, far-reaching and waiting to be undertaken and explored, and that, answers the question, *why writing?*

JENNIPHER M. ZULU

WHERE TO START FROM:

Anyone can write a book; a maid can write a book about how to clean the house, a banker can write a book about financial investments, an entrepreneur can write a book about entrepreneurship, a businessman can write a book on starting and running a business, and an engineer can write a 'How To' book for different innovations and machinery. **Everyone can write a book about something**.

'There's a book in everyone'.... **Elijah Miti**

When I was growing up and eventually got to experience life left, right, and centre; experiencing both the good, as well as the bad, and the highs and lows, I thought to myself that I was quite unique – that my story was very special, which made me feel like my experiences were like none other. Later on, when I travelled abroad for the first time, I had the same feeling about my country. I thought our experiences were unique and that somehow, we had the worst experiences and thus, deserved special attention, pity, and aid. I wanted to tell my story – our stories to the world. I felt like the world needed to know how grave and dire our case was. That they needed to know that we were set apart in a special corner where most of the bad things happened to us only.

This peculiar phenomenon happens to almost everyone. Everyone thinks they are so special at some point – that their story is unique whether in a good way, or bad, and so they feel compelled to tell *their story* – the story that makes them feel unique. For many writers, telling a *unique story* is usually the place where they start their writing journey. In my country, most writers start with a motivational or inspirational book where the author expresses his or her views, thoughts, motivations, and convictions about varying concepts and ideologies. This in itself is a stone thrown not too far from the source. It relates to the personal story theory and that is where most of us seem to stem from.

The assertion that *there is a book in everyone* is thus, affirmed in the above experiences and that is because everyone has a story to tell. A story about the way they see the world and how life, in general, affects them. In case you were still wondering what happened to me, well I learned and now know that when I'm going through a situation, someone out there is either having a much better time than I am or perhaps, they are going through a much bigger problem than I am. When it comes to crossing borders, I learned that we are merely separated by geographical lines and spaces, but much in the same way, face very similar challenges even though our stories may not be the same.

In a quest to get started on a writing project, many authors often ask when the opportune time to start writing is. There are many varying views on this. Others say you need to wait for inspiration, while others advise you to only get started after research on the subject of interest. Better still, others say you need to follow the academic process of plotting, character development, and following a theme. Liberals also add their voices and say that as a writer, you just need to let the story lead you.

All of the above opinions are valid. Writers use different strategies and sometimes, one just needs to stick with what works for them. For example, I start with an idea of what I want to write about. I know where to start from and have a general feeling of where I want to go and most importantly, what I want to communicate across to readers. It is then that I take to research and gather information on the subject matter. The '*how*' unfolds once I start writing. In other words, I mainly work with a theme and the theme helps me build the plot with all its twists and turns.

If you are completely clueless about how to go about writing a book but have a strong desire to do so, there is still a place where you can start from. Like with every other thing that needs to be learned, you can learn how to write a book by looking at how others have done it. Reading a lot of other authors' books is a good starting point in book writing as other people's works show you how ideas are laid out in the genre of your interest, be it poetry, fiction, or non-fiction.

However, reading alone is not enough. Gathering information from other sources like the internet, book clubs, live literary events, and courses go a long way in educating one on book writing. The internet today has endless options with short and long courses available on creative writing... Some are free, while others are paid courses.

There's also a lot of published literature on writing that goes a long way in schooling one to write everything, from book writing, article writing, journal writing, and anything else on writing, giving a vast range of titles on the subject matter. You just have to choose the ones that appeal to you.

CORRECTING THE MISCONCEPTIONS:

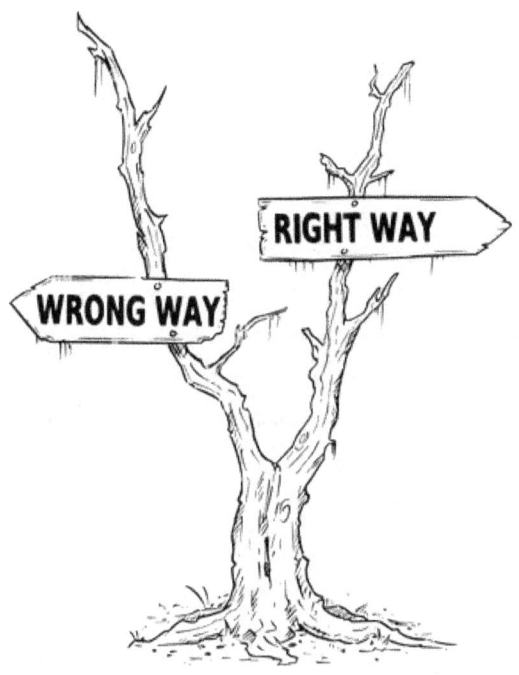

"The biggest misconception about writing is that it's all inspiration and no perspiration."

– Joanne Harris

There are many misconceptions about what it takes to be a writer and what being a successful writer involves. It is important for aspiring writers and those who are just getting into writing to have a well-rounded approach to writing and to have a broad perceptive of what it takes and means to be a writer. Let's look at some of the misconceptions and we will endeavour to correct a few that we can.

Self – Publishing

Self – Publishing is free

Since its inception, the concept of free publishing has not yet been fully understood by many writers and those aspiring alike. For many, with companies like Amazon which offer *'free publishing'* platforms and/or advertise as such, the idea of free publishing is so widely misunderstood that many think *Santa Claus* has decided to extend the holiday giveaways so that they are available all year round. To break it down softly to the sensitive partakers, let me deliver it starting with the definition of publishing, which is another misconstrued process, and then I'll delve into it shortly after.

The word *publish* is closely related to the word *public* and by definition, to publish is to bring, announce, or divulge information to the public. Information, in this case, is not just limited to written work, but it can be images, audio records, or even news delivered verbally. Therefore, the platform used to get your work into the public domain can indeed be free, but the other aspects of the publishing process will still have a cost attached to them.

Amazon, like many other publishing companies, offers a free publishing platform, but you still need to pay for your works to be edited, printed, and marketed. So, it is only one aspect of the publishing process that is usually offered for free in self-publishing and not the entire publishing process.

It's amazing to see some agents advertise, claiming to be offering to publish completely free of charge. However, unbeknownst to the writers, these agents are well aware that other aspects of the publishing process are not free at all. The author only gets to learn of the other costs as they go along.

So know this, the publishing platform can be free, but the other aspects of the publishing process are seldom free.

Self-Publishing is cheaper

Many assert that self–publishing is cheaper as compared to the other forms of publishing. In reality, however, self-publishing does not necessarily mean cheaper.

If a writer wants the very best outcomes, the money to be paid for each stage of the publishing process and the work and effort required to achieve the best outcomes are anything but cheap. Just like any other business, for a high-quality product and great success, a considerable investment is demanded. There is a need for an efficient strategy and considerable efforts to achieve the intended goals.

Self-publishing, however, allows one to break down the publishing process in its individual stages, to be taken up one at a time, rather than taking them up at once as one whole process. In this way, the publishing process is made manageable and affordable, as one can tackle each stage at their convenience when they have the means and resources to do so. The cost of each stage remains the same and may even be more expensive than when taken as a whole. Traditional publishing in this regard may even be cheaper because the cost of each stage is usually subsidised, or offered at a cheaper cost than in self-publishing through agreements and discounts allowed between service providers and publishing houses.

Self–publishing is easy

Many writers and aspiring writers looking to publish their works think that self–publishing is easy. Well, self–publishing has made getting published easy in that aspect, as many manuscripts that would never get to see the light of publishing, now have a route to do just that without the bureaucracy and barriers of traditional publishing with regards to being selected and accepted for publication. With so many self-publishing platforms and means, anyone and anything can get published. I believe that in the past, many good manuscripts were thrown away and many great writers never got to be known or heard of because of the many rejections that were issued by traditional publishing houses when there were no alternative publishing means. The pains of monopolies, right? And sadly, some of those many rejections were based on human preferences and appeal, and not on what it should be; merit without bias.

Even though in the case of traditional publishing, one gets lucky as almost everything that follows after writing a manuscript is taken up and taken care of by other people, in this case, the publishing house. The truth is, very few people get to have their works picked for publication – it's a rough world out there.

Because of the highly competitive nature of traditional publishing, many authors today are opting to self-publish, which has many merits as well as demerits at the same time. Many people have written manuscripts, yet, not all of them see the light of getting published. Most of them get packed away somewhere where they are collecting dust, or where they eventually get lost because the author did not have the finances required to get them self-published.

It should be noted that all the stages of the publishing process are not easy. Take writing, or drafting as an example. Writing requires a lot of engagement mentally, emotionally, and intellectually. It takes so much to draft engaging scripts that people will approve of and end up falling in love with. Not everyone can write stories and tell them so powerfully, beautifully, and convincingly. That is why many say that writing is a gift not given to everyone.

The process of editing is equally very difficult especially because it is often done by an editor who is paid for the job and not by the author. The process requires a lot of involvement, such that it requires one to almost be in tune mentally with the author, to understand what the author was trying to say or express, so that at the end of the process, the best results can be obtained. It is for this reason that the process is very expensive, especially when seasoned and experienced editors are engaged. Professionally, the process is also not delivered by one editor. There are line editors, content editors, developmental editors, and proofreaders; each specialized in a type of editing, yet on the same manuscript. This defines the process as not being an easy one.

All the remaining stages demand a lot of work which includes moving and running around to get things done, talking to different people for services, and going back and forth to ensure everything is working out as required. These are processes that would otherwise be overseen and taken up by the publishing company. But in the case of self–publishing, the writer decides either to do it themselves or hire someone to get the work done. All in all, self–publishing is anything but easy.

Below is a table highlighting a few notable differences and similarities between self-publishing and traditional publishing;

Self – Publishing	*Traditional Publishing*
- The publishing process can be broken down into stages	- The entire publishing process is taken up as one whole process
- Publishing costs can be taken up one by one in correlation to the stages	- Publishing costs are covered as one whole payment, though covered by the publishing company
- Expensive	- Expensive

You just launch out

Of those looking to decide to start writing books, many assume that one just needs to launch out and that's all that is needed. It is good to be optimistic, and I know that many of us have been told that *we need to be risk-takers*, or that *we can never know what is in it unless we launch out*. However, this wisdom has its limitations, places it can be applied, places it can be applied cautiously, and places it shouldn't be applied. One would rightly say 'it's applicable on a case-by-case basis.

In the case of writing, before launching out, one has to take a lot of things into consideration. Initially, one has to take a general study to see what goes into writing, what writing involves, and what it takes for one to successfully write and attain the 'author' or 'writer' title to their name. Next, one needs to do a feasibility study to see if they have what it takes to achieve all that needs to be achieved as a writer and this includes assessing the demands that writing imposes, the necessary skill set needed, the education required, and the commitment that will be demanded. Then, like with any other project, the next step would be putting out a close-to-precise plan of how one will undertake the writing quest including tactics and strategies to be employed. One must never just launch out.

It's all for free

Moving on, we look at dealing and interacting with writers, both locally and internationally. With the knowledge and expertise that I have now acquired, I have received so many requests from aspiring writers and even some writers that are already in the art requesting free services from editing to formatting, to free online publication assistance, and free publishing consultation. There is indeed nothing wrong with helping someone in need, but it is also true that for someone doing business, one cannot help everyone out there. An entity must be a not-for-profit entity and an individual must be doing it for charity to continue offering free services.

Writers need to learn, understand, and accept that there is nothing *free* without a hidden cost, either direct or indirect. Writers must move away from the notion of wanting '*free*' services because, as the saying goes, *even what is said to be 'free' isn't free itself*. There is usually a hidden cost somewhere. For example, in book writing, many writers publish a book and tell you it's free, but you have to pay for shipping. Others say the book is free, but the catch is the downloading costs, and the numbers they reach and convert to customers and followers for future publications.

In book publishing, sites like Amazon offer 'free' publishing platforms but earn from royalties, the authors' own copy purchases, download costs, and shipping costs. With millions of authors accessing the site, Amazon earns its fair share of revenue and profits. Other than the above costs, authors still need to get their works edited, formatted, covers designed, and the book printed. They also need to do a lot of marketing and get reviews for their works to stand out from the millions of other publications on the site. All these services are not '*free*'. Like writing, the services require time, commitment, expertise, and dedication to meet quality standards. Just like authors themselves are looking to gain good income from writing, people offering these services are also looking to gain an income and authors need to understand this and realize that nothing is really '*free*'. Authors need to look at writing as an investment opportunity, the same way they would look at starting any other business.

Whether self-publishing or publishing traditionally, there is a cost that goes with doing so, as has been discussed above. A self-published author is most likely given to bear all costs involved in the publishing process; from editorial costs, formatting costs, cover designing costs, printing costs, and distributional costs, except in the case that they are being sponsored. However, even from this, the costs are only transferred to the third party, who is the sponsor in this case. For traditional publishing, the publishing costs are borne by the publisher who bears all the costs involved in publishing the book project. Therefore, the author must have this in mind when setting out to get their work published.

The actual free publishing

It is possible to write and self-publish your works for free online, as there are many online platforms where people submit works for publication. Calls go out often, for works to be published in magazines, reviews, and many other media forums, although these have recognition motives for the author or authors behind them. By publishing through these media forums, authors are credited by mention, receiving an award, or in other ways. Even though there is still a cost attached to taking this route because writing on its own is costly with time commitment and many other sacrifices made to complete a manuscript. So, it's also not for free.

What then is free publishing?

I'd say, what is referred to as free publishing is a component of the publishing process which is the platform. When they say free publishing, it means they are offering a free publishing platform. That's all unless otherwise mentioned.

Not for the money

Relatively, many people I've met who are either writers themselves, or art promoters in the sector; especially those that are starting, have argued that sometimes writing is not for the money, but is done merely out of passion and love for the art. I quickly identify with them because I was exactly at that same place when I first started as a writer, and then as an art promoter running an organization to help writers in my country. It felt noble and for a good cause to say *I'm just doing it for free*, or *just to help out*. And as a writer, I said I was just doing it for fun, as a hobby, and to breathe, because I had so much passion bubbling from within to bring the words out. Ten years down the line, my story changed. The '*for free'* element changed. Had I suddenly become greedy? No. I guess the answer lies in the reason for your writing.

So, if you are going to just write using pen and paper or a computer, that is a different story, but immediately when you talk about publishing, it becomes a whole new and different story. When you talk about publishing, you have to count the cost, or the cost will force you to consider it.

After years of being on the writing scene; being engaged in various writing-related events and activities, I saw the real need and necessity of money. As a writer, I became drawn to become more professional in the works that I published. The demand for quality became inevitable. With that came the need to consider and source significant investment for my book projects. I found myself seeking sponsors and trying to fundraise on crowdfunding platforms. I continued to do short reads for my family and friends, but even the time to do that subsided. As an art promoter, initially, we wanted many writers to come on board and become members of the organization, of which a good number were drawn. We stuck to minimal affiliation fees and free meetings as much as possible. Upon analysing the needs of the sector after some time, the demand for money to meet arising needs also became eminent. There was no running away from this reality. Writers needed more activities; workshops, meetings, and conferences, which all required money to hire equipment, rent venues, and many other needs. Ultimately, we considered awards, a publishing house, and prize money for writing competitions. But because we were pioneering, getting sponsorship was so difficult and each time, we kept dipping further into our pockets to rise to the occasion. At the end of the day, we simply said, 'like it or not, we need money and thus we need to look into how to make that money.

Aside from the need for actual money, writing demands time, consistency, and commitment to be significant. To give these fully without any monetary reward or gain, one has to consider the many other things that need to be sacrificed during the process. Like in the case of full-time writers, where would money for food, shelter, and security come from during the time the writer is writing?

Therefore, unless a writer just wants to spend very little time writing for fun, or as a hobby, any notch higher than that demands money investment, and '*Not for the Money*' would then not be applicable.

Writing for a name

Most authors launch out writing for a name. They want to be the next Achebe, the next Rowling, or the next Kenneth Kaunda. It is very good to have aspirations in almost everything and it is also very good to have role models. However, in writing, it is also important to have it weighed at the back of your mind that you may not make it to the world's top list, or lists. You may not win many accolades to your name for writing and perhaps, your name may never even be known or heard by many. Nonetheless, you will write for an audience and you will make some book sales. If it is any comfort, suffice to say, *even a bad book has an audience*. Rather than writing for a name as the main focus of your writing venture, it is best that you write for all the other reasons and hopefully, the name comes along.

There are many reasons for one to get into writing. Some of these reasons include writing to educate and inform, writing to communicate, writing for personal satisfaction, writing to make money, and writing for friends. If, however, you are going to opt to write for a name, then you will need to follow the required steps to succeed at doing so. Writing for a name demands hard work, commitment, consistency, sacrifice and above all, a lot of planning and a business approach to writing as a career.

Bogus dreams

The biggest mistake that most local writers make is the issue of having big unrealistic dreams and imaginations about their book projects. When they sit alone at home writing their pieces, they come up with bogus dreams about how people will rush to buy their book in thousands of copies making it a best-seller in no time, and how they will travel the world with their book, and because of their book etcetera. All this is being done without planning and much-needed market research. *Castles built in the air* is what we can allude this to. Of course, it is not disputable, nor arguable that someone can sit home, come up with a very good book idea and it ends up becoming a bestseller, taking them all over the world, but the qualification is that key factors come into play. One has to be a very good writer to pull it off. One perhaps needs to be a very good brand as an author already and coincidentally, or even deliberately, one has to have the right target audience plus other positive factors.

But besides all this, a strategy has to be set in place, a good and feasible plan has to be in place, and all in all, a business approach has to be in force. Otherwise, many writers will suffer from having unrealistic dreams about their books in their heads where they are already famous and have bestsellers and yet, end up flopping in the real world for varying reasons.

The best advice when venturing out in writing is to write with your feet down, single-minded, and with all things considered. Do not allow wild bogus imaginations to delude you. Especially when you are launching out for the first time, keep your expectations at bay; let your first project be a learning point; teaching you the dos and don'ts and perhaps, launch out small the first time because you are testing the waters. If it turns out brilliant, well, and good, and if it turns out the other way, you can learn what you did not do right and what should have been done instead.

One takeaway point writers should have in mind is that there will only be one Chinua Achebe, one J.K. Rowling, one Kenneth Kaunda, and thousands, or millions of other names in the writing world. You may not be any of these names, but you can be yourself, you can write for your audience and you can sell well enough to your available audience.

Printers are thieves claiming to be publishers

There have been many squabbles and claims made about printers parading themselves as publishers and charging writers exorbitant amounts of money in the name of getting their works published. Well, yes, there may be some unscrupulous individuals out there in the industry, laying traps for unsuspecting writers, so they can steal their money. However, let me quickly say that there are printers who are publishers and they fall under the category of Vanity Presses. Vanity presses call for manuscript submissions and request an assessment and publishing fee, paid upfront for the submitted manuscripts. They differ from self-publishers because they take up the publishing process, which is covered in the upfront fee they request for. The most important thing is for the writer to have full knowledge of the different publishing methods and options available because as the saying goes, *'knowledge is power'*. With all the necessary information and knowledge, one can choose wisely.

THE FAIR AND BEST WAY OUT:

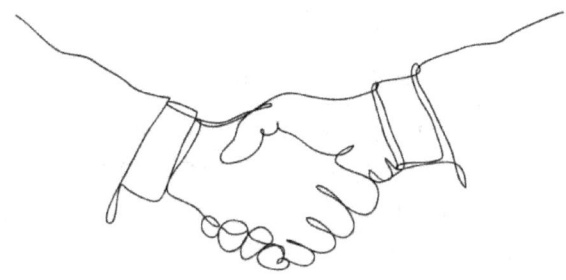

*Justice is the constant and perpetual will to allot to every man his due – **Ulpian***

Considering all the aspects and demands of publishing, printing, distribution, and making actual sales, the best approach a writer can use is one that has been longstanding and has now been modified by online print-on-demand publishers like Amazon Kindle. This is the ***royalty agreement*** approach.

Traditional publishers have from time immemorial used royalty agreements to deal with authors and book publications in general. The author, usually through an agent, is offered a contract by the publishing house, which he/she signs, agreeing to get only a percentage returns from his/her book sales on stipulated terms and conditions. This same approach is now being used by self-publishing platforms where authors get only a percentage of the book sales revenue which is called royalties.

Authors can further adapt the royalty agreement approach to deal with editors, book cover designers, and all other service providers between writing and actual bookselling, rather than requesting free services. This would put on the table *a fair deal* for the author and the service provider for the service rendered. Otherwise, authors would need to re-strategize their book publication project using whatever other means possible, except in cases where the service provider offers a free service out of generosity.

WRITING AS A BUSINESS:

Business

"If a writer wants to significantly earn from their art, they need to start treating it as a business and approach it as such." – **Jennipher M. Zulu**

When many people talk about business, what they have in mind are the typical product and service-oriented businesses and writing is not in mind. Writing is more comfortably seen as a boredom killer or a pastime activity, a stress reliever, a talent-specific activity, and anything else on the side-lines, than a full-time business or career that one can take up and follow in life. However, big-name authors like Mohale Mashigo, MK Asante,

Kayo Chingonyi, Mubanga Kalimamunkweto and many others set writing at a high rank, attracting and inspiring many to follow in their footsteps and today, we see more and more writers pursuing their dreams to become renowned. But if you are among those that are one day looking to publish a book and hope to achieve so much with it, maybe dreaming of taking on writing professionally where you look to mint good returns from book sales, or perhaps you want to take up writing as a career, then you are looking at writing as a business because you will have to do everything that you would ordinarily do in any other business to make your writing career a success.

Start-up principles in writing

When one sets out to start a business, there are a series of requirements and guidelines to meet and follow to successfully establish the business and subsequently, achieve its intended goals. These are called *Start-Up* Principles. In professional writing, the same start-up principles apply in much the same way that they apply when starting any other business because professional writing is a full-time business. Exceptions apply when people decide to write for anything else but professional. Examples include blog writing for fun, social media postings, and writing for friends and self, just for the fun of it.

However, the minute one decides to write professionally, at that point, the approach must change to meet intended revenue goals. There is a need to do some required and necessary assessments and also to plan adequately before launching out and making the investment.

So right here, is the defining point. As a writer, the 'minute' you decide that you want to earn revenue and have an income from your writing, is the minute you should see and approach writing as a business and take the necessary steps. Even if you feel you don't want to realise much from it, the very moment you attach *'revenue'* or *'income'*, treat it as a business.

To set out in your writing business, you initially need to define your required, or necessary processes in business terms. Of course, you will have decided already that you want to write a book, but the first key question is your *'What?'* What do you want to write? Is it a fiction or non-fiction book? What genre? What topic or theme?

Your next question is your *'Who?'* Who is your target audience? In defining your 'who' in writing, you have to cover the age range, preferences, trends, and relevance.

Then you get to your *'When?'* When do you want to start writing? What is your timeframe? Is your writing relevant?

Next, is your *'Where?'* question. Where are you going to get your funds for your writing venture? Where are you going to launch your book? Where are you going to sell your book?

Your last key question is the *'How?'* How are you going to write your book? How are you going to achieve your writing and business objectives? Do you have the necessary skill set? It is in the how question that you should also set out, or write down your writing business plan, covering your selling strategies, advertisement, distribution, and most importantly, your financing plan.

To be more explicit, incorporating all the key questions above, we can say that, one needs to do market research and assess customer preferences. Given all the necessary data, a precise and laid out plan has to be done to map out how the writing project will be done and detail how much investment will be required to implement the plan successfully. Ideally, a revenue forecast then follows for possible and expected returns from the investment. And then, a decision would be made as to whether it is a worthwhile investment or not, the same way it would be done for any other business.

Business management principles in writing

In business management, there are laid down pointers set to help with the smooth running of the business, or venture that helps towards the achievement of the set business goals and objectives. These are called Business Management Principles. For anything that is called a business, these principles are applicable. And when we talk of writing in the business sense, we must also think to apply these business management principles to achieve the writing project's intended goals much more easily than when the principles are not employed. It is easier to see these principles applied in a publishing house because it is an ultimate business entity, with a clear organizational structure and hierarchical workflows.

Many prospective writers and those starting in the art of writing lack this overview of writing. With the insurgence of self-publishing, writing is merely seen as a by-the-way activity that requires very little investment especially moneywise. It is seen as an activity that one just wakes up to and takes up without looking at all the necessary considerations. We can talk about many other principles of business that apply in professional writing, like accounting, planning, marketing, and sales. All of them are well employed in professional writing if the writing venture is to succeed. These principles highlight and indicate the emphasised point that runs pretty much throughout this book. The point is simply that *'professional writing is a business.'*

Looking at it from a detailed point of view, we can see that professional writers and publishers know best to have a business approach to writing. Professional writers have managers, PAs, lawyers, PRs, and other specialists to pay. Their writing career is a full-time business. Publishing houses and other writing-related firms are equally in the writing sector much more for the business aspect of it than anything else. They are in it for the profit and revenue it brings to the table, instead of the selfless acts and the love for the art that they are assumed to be in it for. Many times, their choice of manuscripts to publish is based on the probability of them bringing in huge returns to cover their costs of doing business, for-profit, and for their business to continue running. Therefore, authors must pick a leaf from this and see writing for money as it ought to be seen. From the very beginning, they must approach the idea of writing, publishing, and selling books as a business venture that demands the same requirements and attention that other businesses demand.

Project analysis in writing

The scope of project analysis in writing, like in any other business, incorporates assessing the project's performance as it progresses against the forecasts and goals you set. Although projections for forecasts and analyses are not as easily predictable as in other businesses, some considerations make for good analysis in defining how the writing project should be. For example, feasibility, time, costs, risks, resources, feedback and sales volumes are some metrics used for analysis in a writing project.

Time as a metric in a writing project refers to timelines you set for the project, such as when you need to finish writing, when the editing will be done, when the book will be launched, and when you will have sold your first one thousand copies. A well-planned timeline can significantly contribute to the success of your writing project, ensuring efficient use of resources and timely delivery of your work.

Cost analyses are the cost implications of undertaking the project to its completion and achieving its intended goals. This includes editing, printing, marketing, and distribution costs.

Feasibility assessment help determine whether the project is worth undertaking, continuing or cancelling. A project can be cancelled before it even starts. It can also be cancelled in the middle, and this can be owed to varying reasons like high costs, or not achieving desired outcomes.

Feedback is a key analysis metric as you will be able to know if the project is moving as intended and if it is yielding the desired results.

Research in writing

Before setting out to undertake the writing venture as a writer, you need to make necessary analyses and thereafter, necessary judgments based on gathered data from research, to see if the venture is worth taking, or perhaps analyse what writing venture to even undertake. Research is thus, the bedrock of writing for purposes of revenue.

Market Research

The target audience

1. *The target audience's culture*

Different cultures have different preferences in their reading choice. The kind of stories that appeal to one culture may not be appealing to another culture.

And what is acceptable in one culture, may be offensive and unacceptable in another. One thus has to have in mind the tastes and preferences of the people he/she is writing for, otherwise, the works end up just being for personal entertainment and accolades. Writers need to analyse the market they are writing for, noting the discrepancies in cultures and the people's biases. Imagine writing an erotic book for a Pentecostal church audience. I leave it there.

2. *The target audience trends*

In the writing industry, just like the movie industry, people also like to move with the trends. Recently in the film industry, almost every new Hollywood release, from children's films to adult films, has a touch of magic, wolves, vampires, and Zombies. It's been the '*in-thing*'. The writing industry on the other hand has always been dominated by romance stories, followed by books that provide answers to needs as people would buy these on a need-basis. For example, many *writers* will want to buy this book because of the reality of the challenges faced in the writing industry. Reality and How-To books have also had a big market share. Other big sellers are books on current affairs and high-profile biographies. Talk of Donald Trump and his big American win, and then his leaving office.

Prospecting writers thus, need to analyse the market trends for the target market they want to write for before jumping in to do so. One should keep track of what is trending in all industries. They should take into consideration what is currently selling on the market and what is not.

3. *The target audience's financial capacity*

When I moved to my current neighbourhood, being the business-minded person that I am, I started making cupcakes for a busy neighbourhood shop whose owner was a friend of mine. Upon seeing how busy the shop was, I was so certain the cakes would be sold off like hot cakes in high demand as I planned on using the best irresistible recipes I knew. The first batch I took sold out completely and fast, but not the second, or the third one. Upon seeing the disappointing development, I went to find out why this happened from the shop owner. Soon as we met, he started explaining why it was difficult to sell the cakes before I could even ask him. I guess he was equally discomforted with the development, especially with regard to our good relationship. The shop is right in between a shanty compound and the high-end suburb. He explained that people loved the cakes but the biggest challenge was that, three-quarters of his walk-in customers came from the shanty compound and they preferred things that were priced lower for purchase. They wanted the cupcakes at less than half the price I had pegged them at. Now I thought of the ingredients I used and I knew that either I had to quit or, downgrade to make a reasonable profit. The customers did not consider the value and quality of the cakes I had made, rather they preferred what was affordable to them.

Similarly, it is important to assess the buying capacity of your target audience because for some people, buying a book is a luxury and a waste of resources. In their analysis, it is in their best interest to buy a meal for their family, then allocate money to purchase a book, or perhaps, it is more important to cover their rentals and buy clothing than purchasing a romantic novel.

For such an audience, books that answer needs they have, or provide an immediate solution are more ideal. If you are to write a book after your own heart, then you would have to write it for another audience and you have to consider all necessary costs to do so. Alternatively, writing a book that you will price within their buying capacity would be ideal if feasible.

Product pricing

Product pricing, in this case book pricing is equally a key consideration while doing your market research. Assess how affordable your book will be as compared to other books of a similar volume and genre to yours. For new entrants especially, or let's say, a new author on the block, pricing too high may work against you.

I had always had a problem walking into a local book store and seeing books written by local authors priced way higher than other books in similar categories, or genres. Of course, this wouldn't have been a problem with other factors and influences considered. However, the challenge was that most of the local books were poorly packaged in terms of book build and the materials used were of compromised quality. One would not even question why foreign books were selling more than local ones. These were fancily finished with attractive high-end book covers, good interior paper quality, properly bound, well written, and properly edited. Some were even being sold in combo packs of threes and were still cheaper than one local paperback book.

In writing, you need to take stock of all the costs you will incur to get your finished product, assess how much of a mark-up you will put to make a profit, and set your selling price. However, it is very important to make sure you price right and price competitively. It is a *make-or-break* analysis.

Market penetration strategies

In doing your market research, it is also important to note what market penetrating strategies you will have to employ to penetrate your target market. Comparing the American and UK book markets to African ones will out rightly spell out big discrepancies. For the longest time, most African countries have complained of poor reading cultures amongst the general populace, while in America and the UK, the reading culture is good. So comparatively, bookselling in America and the UK is far much easier than in Africa. These considerations when venturing out are key and assessing what strategies to use to get your book in the hands of the masses and ensuring that it is read are important. At this stage, you look at whether you will use competitions, giveaways, aggressive advertising, book signing events, conferences, motivational speaking opportunities, book discounts, and so on. A good analysis of the target audience will suffice to give you all this information. Other than that, learning from the way others before you are doing it is a great way to go, because you can learn from them what challenges they faced and the strategies they have employed even though experiences may differ with factors considered.

4. Target age range

The target audience age group is another big one when looking at what to write and how to write it. Most certainly, you can't write for a six-year-old child, what you would write for a thirty-year-old adult. There is a big difference because the levels of information analysis, preferences, and information decoding are different. Some rules apply when writing for children as compared to writing for adults and one has to be well conversant with whichever he or she chooses to write.

When doing your market research, you know you want to appeal to your target. If you want to go for economies of scale, you will want to assess which age group is the bigger percentage as compared to the other and work with that.

5. Needs assessment

Most big businessmen and women are people who have capitalised on human needs to provide a solution. Strategic and opportunistic professional writers are those who have learned to do the same. Dr Rozius Siatwaambo is one such author in

Zambia who provided a solution for students, especially those sitting for exams, by writing his bestselling '*Exams Made Easy*' title. From the same title, today he owns a high-profile school, with branches in the capital city and he enjoys great proceeds under the umbrella of the same venture. In the same way, it is important to do a needs assessment of your target audience to write relevant books.

For the longest time, Zambians, in particular, had alluded that the poor reading culture in the country was partly due to the lack of relatable books; that the available books were mostly foreign including those used for academic purposes, like those used in the teaching of literature for instance. Further, Zambians that were attempting to write were writing as though they were non-Zambians and also wrote fictitious places that were non-existent in the country. Yet, the Zambian reading public wanted books about Zambia; Zambian roads, Zambian places, Zambian names, and the Zambian way of life, that they felt they could relate to. This has provided a great opportunity for Zambian writers as there was, and there still is a great need for writers to write stories for Zambians.

The big question when doing a needs assessment is; *what is needed to be written about?*

Content Research

To write on any subject, one has to be very familiar with the subject to be written on. In the case of non-fiction, a lot of fact-based writing has to be employed and this demands a lot of research for one to be familiar with the topic.

Relatively, the question of one having authority on the subject he or she is writing on also comes into play. To have authority on a subject, or topic simply questions the amount of expert knowledge one has on the subject. This expert knowledge may be a personal experience, factual information obtained from reliable sources with adequate backing, or having first-hand information on a subject, etc. This reminds me of what it takes to be a Wikipedia contributor. Posts on Wikipedia can remain pending for a very long time, not until one gets adequate supporting information to back the post. It can be quite frustrating when you feel so strongly that you have the right information as a contributor, and yet you are requested to find more backing information to get your post approved.

Therefore, content research is concerned with what goes into your work/manuscript. What exactly are you going to write about?

Fiction writing also requires familiarity and some level of research unless one comes up with completely imaginary characters like aliens from another planet. But when relating to real-life events, it's ideal to know what one intends to write about. For example, if I want to write scenes involving the police, I should be familiar enough with the way the police operate, some of their rules and regulations, and their basic order of carrying out operations, so that I'm able to write close-to-life scenes that my readers can relate to. Or if one is writing about a court procession, they should be familiar enough with how magistrates, judges, prosecutors, and clerks, carry out their duties in court.

1. Character profile

Of course, many writers have different approaches to how they write, but ideally, as a writer, you ought to pen down a profile for each of your characters, defining them by their character traits and physical appearance. Building each character profile requires research to be done to accurately define your character's reactions, responses, feelings, thoughts, and decision-making. For example, if you have a character who is an astronaut, to accurately build the world around them in your stories, you would need to actually know the real world of an astronaut and not just the one you build from your imagination. It would include the specifics of their work environment, the behaviours of their peers, the influences impacting them, etc. This would require you to either visit their workstations like NASA for example or to extensively research from written works and recordings about them and their environment.

This reminds me of Idris Elba (actor) when he was preparing to play the role of Nelson Mandela. He requested to be put in the same prison cell where Mandela was incarcerated to understand his character and play his role better. This is equally applicable in writing. It is very difficult for some to write about something they know nothing about. Talk about the hashtag *Linton Lies,* which brewed a social media storm around 2016 as readers reacted to Louise Linton's self-published title In *Congo's Shadow*.

2. *Stating Facts*

History writers are best to use as an example on this one. If you are going to write any history, then be sure to write facts. Many people, even in day-to-day life, have gotten in trouble for telling lies. Telling lies is also just plain shameful. History remains the same regardless of how it is twisted or recorded. Here is one fascinating recording; that Dr David

Livingstone discovered Victoria Falls. That is what went down in history books for centuries. Well, the truth is that Dr David Livingstone did not discover Victoria Falls, the locals did. And they used to call it the '*Mosi - O - Tunya*', which means, 'the smoke that thunders'. The right recording should have been, 'Dr David Livingstone was the first white man to visit 'The mighty Victoria Falls' after the locals.

In most non–fiction books including history books, facts have to be stated as they are. Sometimes there are twists and omissions to conceal events like in memoirs and reports, but generally, stating facts is a general rule. To achieve this, especially in cases where the author is a second, or third party in the works being written, the author has to research thoroughly, to present the works factually.

Also, think of a cookery book with mixed-up recipes – that's cooking up a disaster!

The rule is also applicable in fiction writing. Think of someone describing a human being with eight legs, with the ability to fly, and one who's able to eat stones. If you say that's a superhero that would be the right assertion because no normal human being can be like that. Extraordinary - maybe. Therefore, when writing, it must be fact-based and logical.

SWOT Analysis; Self-Assessment

In business terms, this is what would be called a SWOT (Strengths, Weaknesses, Opportunities, and Threats) analysis which is simply the analysis of both the internal and external business environment, and in our case, we are looking at influences that impact the probable success of the book you want to write. The internal environment would be more focused on doing a self-check – looking at you as a writer. The external environment would be everything from outside, that directly, or indirectly impacts the probable success of the book in terms of sales and is widely accepted.

1. Strengths

As a writer, ask yourself what your strengths are. Do you have a writing qualification? What is your writing skill level? Do you perhaps have authority on the subject you want to write on? Are you naturally a talented writer? Are you a good teller of stories in written form even without a qualification? Maybe, you have a good circle of friends that can quickly purchase your first book copies and offer reviews, and perhaps, you have already made a name for yourself in the writing circles, or it may also be that you have a high-profile person to do your foreword and so on.

2. Weaknesses

For weaknesses, it could be that you don't have publishing firms in your country, which means that you have to outsource all the publishing services. Peradventure, you don't have funding or, finances for your writing project. You may also not have your government's support with no implemented book policy, no structures, and operating frameworks to aid you. These impact your project, or may completely impede its success.

3. Opportunities

What are the opportunities available? That is the big question. In analysing what the opportunities are, ask yourself, w*hat the needs assessment findings are and for whichever audience you are writing for*. Asking these questions will help to clarify what you have on the table and what angle to take to salvage it. If analysing from a firm's point of view, look at the demand assessment. How many people want the book publishing service? How many good quality works are being submitted for consideration?

4. Threats

When we talk of threats, we are mainly looking at the existing or, emerging competition. What is your product proposition? Are there other publications with the same theme and goals? How does your work compare against the others?

Also, look at the challenges impacting the business and these may include legal issues with the government which may threaten the closure of the business. For authors, you can look at copyright issues. Many high-profile authors have sued each other over copyright infringement.

THE WRITING BUSINESS
FINANCIAL MANAGEMENT:

"You must gain control over your money or the lack of it will forever control you." — **Dave Ramsey**

Financial management is a very critical component in any form of business. I have seen many great businesses crumble after setting out, not because the proprietor initiators didn't do their homework or research, or didn't have a good enough drive to run with their idea, but they failed because they had poor financial management practices and skills. It is one thing to have a brilliant idea, do all the planning, make the idea crystal and communicate it effectively, but another thing to run it, achieve the set goals and sustain it. In much the same way, I've seen many writers run to the gallery every time they have to run a project. It is always like they are starting over from scratch all the time.

Running a successful writing business employs all the key business principles necessary to run any other business. Managing the finances that come from book sales and other opportunities birthed from the book project is a vital component of determining the soundness of continuing the business. Writers, therefore, need basic financial management skills, covering sales, profit & loss, and inventory analyses. Writers must know, to not eat into the capital required for the next project when spending the money. Decisions on whether to spend, or invest everything back in the business must be carefully made.

The profit analysis must be properly done to keep from operating on loss, whilst assuming that one is making business sense. Relatively, the printing, publishing, marketing, and distribution costs must be analysed carefully, for the same reasons.

A basic understanding of financial management is also important to keep people from stealing from you in case you decide to hire people. As you grow, you may look to have managers, PR people, marketers, salespeople, and distributors. Even in the premise of distributing your works through other vendors, money will not easily be stolen from you if you can do your calculations right.

Financial management also encompasses your focus and discipline to handle and manage your money when it comes from your book sales. Most people fail to remain focused and disciplined once the money comes in. They instead channel that money to other things, until the initial idea dies.

As a writer, you must, therefore, invest in developing your financial skills to gain. Remember, every business runs to make profits, not losses.

PLANNING:

"He who does not plan for success, plans for failure".

If you are looking for significant success in your writing venture, then you can never overlook the importance and necessity of planning for your project.

What you do not plan for, you plan to fail.

From content research, content organization, intended audience analysis, writing time allocation, time frame for book completion, book-selling strategies and tactics, marketing strategies and tactics, finance, sales forecasts, distribution, release date, book launch, etc., everything and every step that goes into writing and bookselling have to be well laid out in terms of planning. Planning is an important step for any activity and endeavour for several reasons.

Time aspect

Zambia won the AFCON 2012 trophy. In the short period before and after the AFCON, the Zambian football jersey sold for millions. It was actually sold out in many sporting shops and when found, it was very expensive. Many fans cared little about the cost; they were buying *'in the moment'*. It was a thing about pride, identity and association. But in the long term, the price declined and so did demand.

In writing, many times themes are relevant to a specific period beyond which the relevance subsides. Certain writings are only relevant to a prevailing situation and should be published on a needs basis. If you are going to write in response, or in line with an event, time is of the essence, you need to plan your writing in such a way that you set workable systems and adopt writing habits that ensure your works are written as and when you need to write and publish them.

Moving with the trends

Relatively, the relevance of a written work can be well married to the prevailing trends. For example, in recent times, most Hollywood movies for teens have a touch of magic, zombies and wolves. This is what is trending. And to be relevant, most filmmakers have to conform to and incorporate the trending factors in their scripts and production. The same rule applies to writing. In planning your work, you must, therefore, pay attention to the prevailing trends in the writing industry. Learn what your target audience is mostly running for.

Plan your book events

Everything you accord due time and effort in terms of planning is highly likely to yield desired results. Book signings and book launches are all areas that need key planning that includes budgeting, logistics, and administration. If you don't plan well, say you miss the opportune time, it means fewer book sales will be made and most likely, losses will be incurred, because you will have already spent on other event-related costs.

Meeting deadlines

Especially when it comes to professional writing, meeting deadlines is a big issue. Writers commit to churning out manuscripts according to set agreements. Otherwise, missed deadlines would mean missed opportunities. The need to do precise planning becomes very apparent in order to balance things and ensure a smooth workflow and fulfilled objectives.

If you don't plan your writing to meet agreed deadlines and also put in the required effort towards meeting those deadlines, then you are already planning to fail. You will probably end up with fewer book products to sell per period, fewer, or even no returns. It's better luck next time.

Established writers' activities and events

You might want to take into serious consideration, what established writers are doing during the time you are planning to launch your book. Include icons on this one. Imagine a book written for a renowned influencer being released at the same time as you. You risk your book events being choked out of the limelight before your book is even noticed.

Find what works for you

In planning your writing time and strategies, it is always key to find what works for you, and not what is standard for many. Many who have tried to copy what others are doing have gone on to launch out and fail in the end. This is because what works for others may not work for you.

Whatever strategies you decide to use, must be strategies you have tried and mastered in order to leverage the opportunities you have at hand. Trying anything you have never tried may require expert knowledge for implementation, without which, challenges may be encountered, and in the end, failure may be the outcome.

THE WRITING BUSINESS PLAN TEMPLATES:

In business, different types of plans are used for the sound functionality of a business. In an entity, every department of the business employs the use of a specifically tailored plan to meet its needs per period. However, a general business plan or, the overall plan is usually prepared from the onset of the business and is updated regularly as needs change, or as milestones are achieved. A business plan takes on many forms and is specific to the nature and type of the business entity.

1. *The writing business plan*

In writing, the business plan is and should likewise be tailored specifically to meet the needs and scope of the writing business. For our reference, let's therefore, call our business plan, *'the writing business plan'*.

The writing business plan is a very important facet in the writing business and as mentioned above, is required right at the beginning of the venture and before the actual investment is done, just like in other businesses. A good writing business plan will guide you through each stage of starting and managing your writing business. The plan will help you see what kind of help you need, from whom, or what skill is required to engage in your venture. It will help you to think through and detail all the key elements of how your writing business will run.

The general business plan is usually written as a three to five years projection of the business outlining the path the business intends to take to earn and grow revenue. In our case, we'll settle for three years, considering the nature of the business.

The writing business plan can be looked at as a living and functional document of your writing business. Ideally, the plan is further broken down into sales, marketing, pricing, operations, PR and distribution, and whatever other component is necessary and applicable.

Your calendar of events and activities for your writing venture can also be broken down and analysed as milestones to be achieved along the business plan timeline. This can also be looked at as an action plan.

Step 1: Background

A single, clear, compelling message that states why you are different and why you are worth the attention – **Steve Blank**

Your background is the hook and bait to possible funders and sponsors. It needs to be hooking enough and at the same time, compelling and convincing that your work is very necessary. In typical business plans, this is what is referred to as the *'Executive Summary'*.

Step 2: Define your writing objectives

Many people set out to write for varying reasons, but there are three basic reasons why people write. First is persuasion, second is entertainment and third is to inform. These three reasons also fall under two categories. Either one writes for fun, or business. The two categories further define writers in categories of those who write to make a name for themselves; those who take writing as a hobby – a pass-time activity; those who write for friends; those who write to compete to prove themselves against their perceived rivals; those who write to communicate a message, share their opinion, or analysis on a subject; and lastly those who write as a lifetime career and a business venture.

Your writing objectives must be clearly stated right from the beginning to help you map out a precise course of action in your writing venture. In other words, as a writer, or an aspiring one, the day you decide to venture into writing, you must know exactly why you want to write. Knowing your motivation to write helps you get a direction of how you are to launch out in your writing journey.

Your writing objectives can be laid out in bullet form if you like and they can include raising a specific amount of money for yourself or charity. Note that, in specifying your objectives, there is nothing wrong with saying you are raising money for yourself, which translates into self-empowerment. You can also state a problem you are addressing or highlight a societal problem.

By stating your objectives, you will know how much investment will be required of you to commit towards your writing venture.

Step 3: The Swot Analysis

When the writing objectives are clear and stated, the next step is the detail of your Swot analysis which has already been dised above, giving an overview of your venture positioning. The information you share here is from a precise analysis of your strengths, your weaknesses, your opportunities, and your threats. You would have assessed what needs to be done to leverage the grey areas highlighted if possible. You can thus state here what vantage points or areas you have, including your writing authority on the subject matter and what experience and skills you may have.

Step 4: Operations - Strategies and tactics

The next step is detailing your strategies and tactics. How do you plan on undertaking the whole project? What strategies and tactics are you going to use to reach the masses and achieve your specific goals and objectives? What steps are you going to take? Also incorporate here, a timeline of activities for the events you will specify.

Step 5: Marketing (telling your story)

In business terms, marketing is in simple terms, defined as telling your story. Here, you define your product. What are you offering? What is its promise? How is it packaged?

Marketing includes marketing materials that you will be selling like T-shirts, caps, mugs, pens, bookmarks, speaking engagements, interviews you will be paid for, etc. After defining your product, state how you will spread the word about it. What advertising methods are you going to use? What branding efforts are you going to incorporate? This includes banners, pull-ups, fliers, etc.

Step 6: Financials

Under financials, specify how much will be needed for each activity. Also, specify how much will go to advertising, marketing, logistics, and administration. What is the total budget? These may just be approximate figures, but try to make them as close to the actuals as possible.

Under financials, also write your sales projections. In writing, what I have experienced is that book sales are more in the first year when the book has just been published, and then the sales start to decline over time. So, have that in mind when making your projections.

Example of a writing business plan

Background:

- There are few records of the several events that took place during the struggle for Zambia's independence. There is a need for more documentaries, films, and writing to depict the events at the time. This novel will be the first written in its format, for purposes of recording, educating, and passing on information, especially to future generations, about the events of the time.
- The author of the book has carried out a four-year extensive research on the subject, collecting key information on actual events that took place during the said time, consulting surviving freedom fighters, visiting libraries and government archives, and also visiting stations for archived footage relating to the same.

Objectives:

- To write a novel detailing key events that affected the nation during the independence struggles of then Rhodesia.
- Sell one thousand copies in one month and a total of one million over the next three years

SWOT analysis:

Strengths:

- The author holds an MA in Literature which gives him a competitive advantage and quality assurance.
- The project is the author's second book so he has experience.
- His first book was a bestseller with 5,600 copies sold in six months.
- The author's name sells itself after the success of his previous project.

Weaknesses:

- No available finances at hand.
- Have to outsource editing, graphic designing, and distribution services which impose a higher cost of getting the books ready thereby reducing expected revenue.

Opportunities:

- Five book clubs awaiting the release of the book in order to purchase 50 copies each.
- Government policy review now allows for ten copies of every author's published book to be purchased for each school as long as the book meets set standards.

- Availability of loyal customers to purchase up to three hundred books.
- Distribution through bookstores dotted around the country.

Operations - Strategies and tactics

- Three companies that are ready to assist with book distribution are waiting for the book to be released after being given notification of the book project. The author is thus, set to make these advance sales and also use these sales as advertising bait for more sales
- Planned adverts on all media to boost awareness and sales.
- Book signing plans in all provinces.
- Distribution in all schools.
- Seek approval for the book to be used for teaching in schools which will increase purchases and for a longer period.
- Distribution through bookstores.

Financials

Expenses:

	Quantity	Cost
Book editing		K 7000
Book printing	1000	K 60000
Distribution		K 20000

Advertising		K 8000
Book launch		K 25000
Totals		**K120000**

Sales Projections:

	Year 1	Year 2	Year 3
Books	800000	600000	300000
T.Shirts	5000	3000	1500
Laptop Bags	4500	3800	2900
Speaking Engagements	4000	3500	3000
Totals	**K813500**	**K 610300**	**K 307400**

To make the jargon above more palatable I'd say when you set out to write, also have in mind how much it will cost you to publish your book, the number of copies to print, how much you intend to peg your book price per copy (factoring in bulk purchases and other price influencers), what strategies you will use to make sure that you make good book sales, and also your target audience.

The sales plan

The sales plan is an important component of a successful writing business, especially in this era of self-publishing. I have seen many self-published authors with good books that end up being stuck with a pile of printed copies of their books, with nowhere to take them and not knowing what to do with them. Having a good sales plan and being able to successfully implement it and yield good returns with it is the ultimate success. Some of the renowned authors known around the world who have sold millions of their book copies have achieved this by having a great sales plan.

The sales plan is all about projections in terms of sales and revenue and also strategies to achieve those projections. It is not enough to set targets of how many books you want to sell. You also need to know how you are going to sell those books towards the set targets and through what means. Some authors I know use their other talents to sell their books. A good example is public speaking. Public speakers who also write on the side use their speaking engagements to sell their books. Recently in Zambia, Dumisani Ncube sold thousands of his first title using his public speaking influence.

The sales plan also details the marketing strategies that will be employed to publicise the book. For example, advertising through various media, conferences, marketing materials, etc. Putting together a sound sales plan takes into consideration many factors, including detailed research of the target market and other impacting external factors. For example, a targeted market with people going through a recession may impact book sales as people change their priorities, prioritizing more necessity goods than luxury goods, in which category many people put books. In such an economy, one needs strategies for market penetration, like writing a book that provides a solution to a problem, or how to run an online business rather than one that only entertains.

As a writer, you must, therefore, think of everything that might possibly impact your sales projections in order to formulate precise tactics and strategies to achieve your projections.

THE WRITING INDUSTRY:

The writing industry has many facets, offering many different opportunities to writers and other professions. Writers and others working in writing-related fields create linkages with people from other formal working fields, making it a fully functioning industry.

These linkages either feed directly, or indirectly into, or out of other businesses and thereby, making a whole industry. Below is a simple illustration showing some of the businesses that feed into, or from writing.

Fig. Examples of entities that benefit from writing

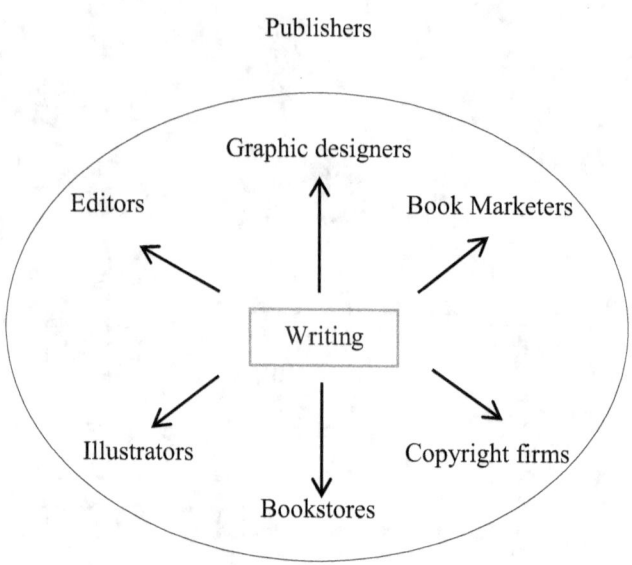

In countries where the writing industry is well established, funding is set aside from governments, non–profit organizations, and the private sector, with governments setting aside budget allocations towards the sector to keep it afloat and fully functional. Policies and support structures are well defined, ensuring the performance of the sectors.

Revenue brought in by the sectors contributes towards the countries' Gross Domestic Product and forex from international purchases and shipping costs. The sectors are well appreciated and considered as having a big influence on other sectors like culture and tourism.

The writing industry more specifically, creates employment and opportunities for other professions including marketers, lawyers, distributors, accountants, sales personnel, graphic designers, illustrators, editors, reviewers, and TV and radio stations, which are all professions that stand to benefit from an established writing industry.

The writing industry's importance cannot be overemphasised. A good example is the recent happenings in Zambia. Zambia lost its founding father, the country's first president, Dr David Kaunda, popularly known as KK. The event showed how little documentation has been done on a man who not only fought for the country's independence but also for the neighbouring countries. He was an icon, greatly revered for the efforts he made during the independence struggle in the region, one who was mourned worldwide. Therefore, it is clear to see why the industry needs good investment because too much information is lost when the industry is not established and documentation is not properly and adequately done.

Even though a well-developed writing industry has so much to offer in terms of opportunities, in many countries, especially developing countries, the writing industry is overlooked and left underdeveloped if it exists at all. Studies have indicated that the major factor causing this state of affairs is the lack of political will from the leaders in the country. With the global challenge of unemployment, an underdeveloped or side-lined writing industry only goes to the detriment of a nation and is also a failure by governments to utilize a dormant opportunity to their advantage.

Entities in the writing industry

There are many entities that operate in the book industry (writing and publishing) and these include;

Editing Firms

Book reviewing firms

Graphic designers

Printers

Publishing firms

Illustrators

Understanding the value that writing brings to society and the economy, helps to give a better perspective of the industry's offering.

OPPORTUNITIES IN THE WRITING INDUSTRY:

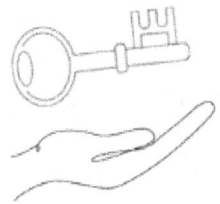

A well-established writing industry offers many opportunities for writers and other professions alike. In the business and professional world, companies employ writers for various roles including research writing, report writing, underwriting, copywriting, editing, etcetera. Writers are also hired for business writing, to write content for marketing, e.g., flyers, and business profiles, to communicate and define brands, and to write content to communicate company values and offering to the target market via various media.

Opportunities for writers

Writing on its own also offers many opportunities as there is just so much going on everywhere around us, with so many events and information to record for future reference, for history keeping, communication, and teaching purposes. For entertainment purposes, there are just so many stories to write, both fictitious and true-life stories, offering writers a range of opportunities with millions of books being distributed worldwide, giving writers millions of dollars to bag for their authored books. In this way, writing offers a lucrative career and income generator.

Writers also benefit from offering writing services for which they are paid money to get the work done. People hire writers for these services because they are not graced with the writing skill as writers are, and sometimes because, they just don't have the time to write themselves and so they engage writers to do the writing for them. This is ghost writing. Ghost writers are writers who write on behalf of clients and the work is read as if the clients wrote it themselves. In this case, clients avail the writer with all the information they want to be written for them and then the writer works their magic, transcribing the information into the complete written work desired. The client's name is then appended to the work as if it was written by them, while the writer's benefit is a fat check.

Others write their work the best they can themselves, then they engage a writer to organize it, adding and subtracting where possible. The writer is then paid their due for their contribution. I'm not so sure how to categorize these because I do not want to entirely put them in the ghost-writing category, but what I know for certain is that they make a fat get-away with decent pay for getting the work done. I'm talking about university students, former university students, and just players with a wealth of knowledge in a particular field, who write dissertation papers on behalf of students who either feel too lazy to do it themselves or just lack the know-how of doing the work. It's called cheating, but the writer makes good money from it; or is it bad money?

Writers are also paid for private engagements such as article writing and being contributors to anthologies, magazines, and writing reports for newspapers. In most cases, payment is per story or, per word count in the contributing piece.

Opportunities for non- writers

The writing industry offers numerous opportunities not only for writers but also for various other professionals. From my experience in writing and publishing, I had to engage multiple service providers to transform my work from draft to published work, encompassing the entire publishing process.

Between "draft" and "published work," several key players are involved: the editor, proofreader, reviewer, typesetter, graphic designer, and publisher. Post-publishing, the marketer, distributor, seller, and reprographic rights protector, play crucial roles.

The writing industry provides ample opportunities for other professions to establish businesses that serve writers, or that are literary related. For instance, marketing professionals can create firms dedicated to marketing literary products and services. A notable example is *Hazel Online*, which markets and sells Zambian books online. Internationally, *Kirkus Reviews* stands out in the reviewers' category, while locally, *Majorie's Book Reviews* and *White Lake Reviews* are significant.

Book Reviewing

Established book reviewers can earn significantly from authors who seek validation, credibility, and visibility for their work. The minimum fee for a review from Kirkus Reviews is $399. Although writers may opt out of reviews, professional editing is indispensable.

Editing

Once a writer finishes drafting, the next step is editing. In Zambia, editing costs range from K3500 to K25000, with some packages including publishing. Internationally, editing prices start from

$1500. Editors can establish firms and secure a substantial stake in the industry.

Graphic Designers

No book is complete without a cover. Whether in soft copy, paperback, or hard copy, a professionally designed cover significantly impacts book sales by attracting prospective buyers. Beyond book covers, graphic designers can offer ad graphics and video trailer services.

Reprographic Rights and Legal Services

Entities like the Zambia Reprographic Rights Organization (ZARRSO) protect authors' works from unauthorized reproduction. Additionally, lawyers can provide legal services for plagiarism cases, ensuring authors' rights are protected.

The Government

The government also benefits significantly from an established writing industry through taxes and statutory fees. Therefore, it should invest in the industry to ensure optimal functioning and maximize its earnings.

The various facets of the writing industry are crucial, highlighting the essential nature of writing. The opportunities extend beyond writers, making the sector a fertile ground for multiple professionals to thrive.

THE WRITING BUSINESS
UNDERSTANDING BOOK PUBLISHING:

What is publishing?

We earlier defined publishing and we said; the word *publish* is closely related to the word *public* and by definition, to publish is to bring, announce, or divulge information to the public, and that information, in this case, is not just limited to written work, but it can be images, audio records, or even news delivered verbally.

There are many ways to publish and get published. As long as your work is brought to the public, the medium used is the publishing channel.

What are the publishing methods available?

Traditional Publishing

Old school Publishing is what we might as well call it. Traditional publishing is quite old. In the *Shakespearean* time, traditional publishing was the only available method of publishing. It was 'either you get your manuscript accepted or, your book is out!'

Traditional publishing requires you to apply for publication either directly or through an agent. The latter is preferred. Normally, publishing houses would call for manuscript submissions. This is done during their submission windows. You would have to attach a cover letter to your application and submit a sample of your work that conforms to communicated specifications. Once accepted, the publisher then takes up the remaining stages of the publishing process. If rejected, you would get a notification to that effect, unless prior advice stated that you would not be communicated to. This is usually due to high volumes of submissions.

Vanity Presses

Vanity Presses are also a very old practice where the publisher requests money upfront to assess the manuscript and publish it. We discussed them earlier. Perhaps also note that Vanity Presses are not so selective on manuscripts they publish. They simply publish anything they accept.

Self - Publishing

Self – Publishing is self-explanatory. The writer in this case takes up all the stages of the publishing process and meets the financial obligations attached on their own, or by sponsorship.

Self – Publishing Print – On–Demand

Print on demand can be a hybrid of self-publishing and vanity press. As a writer, you can take up the entire publishing process, but when it comes to printing, you can engage a printing company where you only print copies as or when you need them. You can also print according to orders received. Thus, the term print-on-demand. Alternatively, you could opt to engage a company to take up the entire process and only purchase your copies

The publishing process

I remember the first time I wanted to publish my book, I was so elated at having finished my draft. I had spent a few good sleepless nights at that, penning all my thoughts to paper, and yes, I didn't even have a laptop at the time. However, you know how things just tend to work out and fall into place. I was just one year old in marriage by then. As our tradition has it, I had very few things to my name and the things my husband got for me since we married.

My husband had a laptop and for two days at least, I didn't give him peace. I worked on transferring my paperwork to the laptop every little chance I got. Soon as I was done, I started my search for a publisher. I was so determined that nothing could have dissuaded me.

As my memory would have it, a few names of publishers I had come across came to mind and these were Mission Press, Maiden Publishers, and Macmillan Zambia. I sent emails to Mission Press and Macmillan Zambia, to which I never received any reply to date. I went to Maiden Publishers in person and the reception was nothing close to being pleasant. The lady that received me never even offered me a seat. She looked at me from head to toe after I presented my case and coldly told me that the company doesn't publish local writers. I was heartbroken, but that did not deter me. I went home, hoping to receive feedback from the other two publishers.

While waiting, I decided to start searching for publishers online and that's how I came across Lulu Publishers (UK) and Createspace Publishers (USA). Createspace was even offering free shipping for the proof copy when you published with them. I jumped on the opportunity and that's how I got published.

However, I'll tell you, that what I published was very raw and needed a lot of work. Firstly, I made very little attempt to edit the work. My primary goal was just to get the work published. I learned the right way of doing things the hard way.

Leaning on my experience, here are the stages of the publishing process. Ensure to adequately see your work through all the stages for the best outcome of your project.

The publishing process can be broken down into nine distinct stages as indicated below;

Stage 1 - Research stage

Stage 2 - Writing

Stage 3 - Editing

Stage 4 - Formatting

Stage 5 - Interior and cover design

Stage 6 - Printing

Stage 7 – Public presentation

Stage 8 - Marketing

Stage 9 - Distribution and sales

Each of the above nine stages of the process has its cost implication and imposes its challenges to the process.

The research stage is the first stage which involves gathering data from various sources. This data can be information for character development, or anything that helps to give your work a backbone and firm foundation. It could also be the stage you are putting your ideas together and organizing how you want them to flow. In the case of non-fiction, you can talk about gathering facts about what you want to write about.

The writing stage is the stage when you are doing the actual writing, and penning down the ideas, thoughts, and data you have collected at the research stage. You can write and complete your first draft and then start the editing part to come up with subsequent drafts. How many drafts you can do before going to the next stage is determined by different factors. The work can even return from the next stage to be re-drafted as a subsequent draft.

The writing stage can be anything from easy to difficult. If you are writing from your own knowledge and experience, it can be quite easy, but if you are writing other kinds of writing, the stage can be quite technical and difficult.

The editing stage is the third stage, one that I consider being quite difficult. As a writer, it is difficult to fish out your errors, let alone even see them. You can read half or incomplete sentences with missing words so many times, and each time, read them as though they were complete sentences without you realizing it. A fresh pair of eyes is always best to comb through your drafts. A professional editor, or perhaps editors, since there are different types of editing, can be engaged to get the job done.

Editing is very important in book publishing and it can mean everything for a book's success, or failure. Readers and critics sometimes trash works they consider poorly edited and unfortunately, a book with great potential can be trashed before it is fully read, based on the extent of editing work that was done, or that requires to be done.

Stages 4 and 5 can be taken up together because they entail, the complete packaging of the book, both inside and outside. Formatting in book publishing simply means organizing your book and that encompasses the layout, fonts, style, cover designs, and technical specifications of the interior and exterior files.

Printing is the stage that follows after formatting and cover design. And like subsequent stages, it is pretty much obvious and straightforward. You simply shop around before settling for a printer of choice, based on your considered factors like price, quality, and package offered.

Now, stage 8 can almost fall anywhere and not only where it has been placed. You can opt to start marketing your book even before you start writing. This especially works best for renowned writers and writers who publish regularly. You can also choose to market your book way after publishing and selling your first few copies. You can also market it in the middle of the publishing process as listed above. This can create a surge of anticipation for your book.

When opting for the self–publishing method you can take up the stages, one stage at a time, as earlier alluded to. In this way, you can strategically raise money for one stage at a time if you so wish, making the process manageable and affordable because it will be at your own pace and convenience.

JENNIPHER M. ZULU
WRITING AS A SIDE-HUSTLE:

A side-hustle is the new job security - **Forbes**

With the imminent need for more jobs to be created and for workers to have more than one stream of income, having a side hustle is now more of a necessity than an option. That being the case, writing makes for a good option to invest in when one has the right target audience and the right literature to offer. While keeping that much-needed job, one can also be a very successful writer, writing only in the time gaps when away from work. And that is the beauty of writing.

Writing can be done anywhere and at any time as long as one can do so. The only downside to it is that adding writing to an active career means more work and less rest. However, if one takes writing as a hobby, a stress reliever, a breather, and anything else other than work, it turns out more rewarding, overshadowing the perception of it being work. This can be done by analysing your need to write or, the reason why you want to write, aside from making money from it.

In giving examples, let me first emphasize the importance of always trying to write within one's area of interest, or genre. This is very important as it makes the process of writing easier because one will be able to derive pleasure and fulfilment whilst getting the work done. You can add writing in the area of one's experience and expertise to that list.

When you are writing in your area of experience or expertise, information flows from your knowledge base. You don't have to do so much research for the work, although research is always necessary.

Let's take the example of writing a memoir about some experience you had. Let's say the main reason you are writing that memoir is to convey some information, or knowledge you believe is very important to your target audience. When writing this memoir, your motivation, or intention will be the lead and drive. You won't want to stop writing until you feel you have successfully emptied that motivation, or bled that motivation on paper.

We can use another example of you writing a narration of a trip you took some years back. You will passionately detail your experience, leaving out only that which you feel is not necessary, or not for public consumption, and you will do so to the last detail. In this way, the work won't feel like work at all. Other examples we can look at are; profiling an influential person, recording a significant event to the last detail, sharing 'how-to' knowledge, and telling your life story. If you will write as a service, try to stick to a genre you enjoy, or are comfortable with. In other words, only accept work that piques your interest, unless you have the grace and capacity to tackle other genres.

Writing to complement one's business or expertise is another great avenue for extra income. Zambia's Bruce Sikombe, *the Customer Service Scientist,* is a good example of someone using his expert and professional knowledge in tangent with writing to advance his career and service provision. Bruce has successfully organized and hosted the annual Customer Service Summit, for which he also prepares written materials in book form, which he sells per participant.

Another example we can cite is Isaac Pomboloka, the host of the ADEPT Summit/Book/Awards event.

The last example is Dumisani L. Ncube, the Radical Entrepreneur who hosts the Africa Must Think Summit, a platform that encourages critical thinking and innovation in business. Dumisani's written materials for the summit have enhanced the event's quality and significantly contributed to his brand and service provision, demonstrating the power of writing in advancing one's professional journey.

Writing for magazines, and journals, submitting to anthologies, and article and report writing, are alternatives that offer incentives for one taking writing as a side hustle. Many calls offer payment per number of words and most often, per story, or submission as stated above. In these hard times we are in with most economies grappling for stability, very few people can throw away an opportunity for extra income. You can make extra money from your book sales or offer writing services as a side-hustle.

WHAT TO WRITE:

At this point, if all you have read makes business sense, and you've thought to yourself, 'ok, I think I can try to write as a business, or I can try to write for business purposes, and then you further ask yourself, *'what then will I write?'* Well, there is a vast range of options to choose from. It all depends on what piques your interest and the reason why you feel you should write. There is everything to write about. Every activity, event, and object under the sun is worth writing about and that is a very wide range. There is the recording of events as history and for reference, report and narrative writing for news and past events, and writing for teaching purposes like cookery books and academic writing. When we talk of fiction writing, the options are unlimited because we see and decode things and information differently, even when we go through the same experience. Let's delve in a little further;

Memoirs/Biographies

If you are a person whose life has made a notable impact on society, are outstanding with a life that stands out; a life many people would want to learn from, then you can choose to write an autobiography about yourself. If you are an author offering a service in this regard, then you can write an autobiography for an outstanding and notable figure. If the person you are writing about is late, then that will be called a memoir, or biography.

One thing you need to be mindful of when writing either a biography or an autobiography is that your writing must be fact-based. If you are writing about your own life, a lot of information about you may already be in the public domain, so you must have that in mind and make sure it aligns unless it's a correction. If you are writing for a notable person, or about a notable person, make sure you do your homework to research extensively so that you get all the facts right.

Event records

When our founding father, Dr Kenneth Kaunda (Zambia) died, we saw the many gaps in the undocumented events, including details of the struggle for independence. Many other significant events have gone undocumented, leaving so many gaps in our historical records. The country and the world at large need things happening around us to be recorded for future reference, for memory, or history, and as a means of passing on key information to future generations. In the case of history, people always want to know where they are coming from, how things were done in the past, how people were living, or how certain events happened and the effect they had on the affected people. Today, scientists dedicate their whole lives, trying hard as they can to track cultures and ways of life. Suffice, therefore to say, recording events is very important.

Apart from history, other forms of information can also be recorded and passed on through written records. For instance, a family tree can be documented and passed to subsequent generations of a family who continue to add to it image inserts. Outstanding events can also be documented, like accounts of the Mailon brothers in Zambia, the Lenshina Uprising, Zambia's contribution to Rhodesia's Bush War, past democratic elections, Dr Kenneth Kaunda's ousting, gassing incidences of 2020, the AFCON 2012 win for Zambia, ritual killings of 2019, music concerts, conferences, summits, etcetera.

How-to Books

Cookbooks, guides, and other '*How to'* *books*, all fall under this category.

Expert knowledge can be written with the intent to teach and guide the target audience on how to do certain things, or how to carry out certain processes and activities. A typical example we can consider are cookbooks. Cookbooks detail step-by-step cooking recipes for various foods and delicacies. The details are stated precisely such that when followed through, the end-user gets the exact cooking result as described and presented in the cookbook.

How-to books are unlimited. One can write about how to become a soldier, how to fly a plane, how to chop down a tree, how to win betting games, how to propose marriage, how to start up a business, how to run a successful business, and the list goes on and on. We can thus, see that 'how-to' books convey knowledge to the reader on how to do things.

The best people to write how-to books are people with expert knowledge on the subject, or topic to be written on, or people with authority on the subject, either by experience, or extensive research. How-to books are also fact-based writings. The minute information is twisted, outcomes are not to be as expected as described. Imagine a guide on how to assemble a table having mumble-jumbled information and even some of it missing. That table cannot be assembled except with accurate guesswork.

Reports, articles, and essays

You can opt to write articles and essays, give your opinion on a subject or write reports of your research findings. These are usually submitted to newspapers, journals, and magazines, which may, or may not directly pay you, but perhaps through other means, like having a dedicated column, contributor privileges, and publicity.

There is a thin line between articles and essays, the major distinction being that one is objective, while the other is subjective. Articles are written more objectively, citing, referencing, and borrowing the ideas of others, while essays are subjective, expressing the opinion of the author alone.

Reports, articles, and essays range from short write-ups with a few pages to long ones, up to ten pages or more. You can write reports, giving accounts of incidences in your community such as murder, rape, mob justice, etcetera. You can even write articles on prostitution in your area, street life for the homeless, the impact of empowerment programs, etcetera.

Fiction

Calling on imaginative thinking, yes, this is it. Here we can let our minds wander and create worlds and characters as seen in Lord of the Rings, Harry Potter, The Neighbors, Buk, and so on. These are all a product of imaginative writing. A disclaimer is usually written in fiction books that any resemblance to real-life characters is but by mere coincidence.'

Fiction writing can be fun and can carry you on a roller coaster of emotions as you write. Sad scenes can make you cry, while happy and exciting ones can make you laugh out loud. And the good side to all this is that when your work is done, it can be sold to earn you money.

You can also offer fiction writing as a service or write clients' stories as a ghostwriter. Ghostwriting can fetch big revenue, especially when writing for high-profile clients. You can also earn from fiction writing by contributing to short story anthologies and also submitting to magazines and competitions offering prize money, or just payment per story or, per number of words.

Non-Fiction

When Mizinga Melu gives an account of her life so far, detailing the challenges she faced and overcame, the wins and highs, etc - this would fall under the non-fiction category. When you decide to write on Africa's challenges and opportunities, it is also non-fiction. And then, we have motivational books, which are the most common in this category.

Non–fiction books can fetch a fortune and can be a game-changer for the author as well. There are many success stories of writers who rode on the success of their books and with them, went on to do great things. In Zambia we have Dr Rozious Siatwambo who used his title, '*Exams Made Easy*' highlighted earlier, to achieve so much to his name today. We also have Mubita C. Nawa who was the first motivational speaker who used his writing and motivational speaking to achieve a lot today.

"When you have lived a successful life, there comes a point when you just need to stop, look back and start sharing what you have learned to do right, with those coming behind you."

...Tony Elumelu

On who should write, my passion resonates with the above quote for those that have made a mark in life.

There are just too many people in the world and each one is fighting to overcome various challenges, hurdles, and setbacks, trying everything they can, to figure out life's success secrets. It is, therefore, necessary for those that have learned the secrets, to pass them on to subsequent generations. And what better way to do so than by putting it in a book?

A book lives through many lifetimes, outliving even the author, and all the way, disseminating its reserves through the pages. Today we all know Einstein's formulae because they were written down a long time ago. The great fellow has been dead for decades and yet, his knowledge continues to transcend time, educating today's generation and will educate tomorrow's.

People should also take up the challenge to write merely because there is a need to write. Take, for instance, writing children's books and academic books. These are necessary and required books, for teaching, and without which, there would be such a gap in the system. Books should thus be written by everyone as long as they have something to share. A father's note to the son, a sole proprietor to his/her children, a leader to the community, a pastor, a businessman, a mother and simply put, anyone and everyone who has passion. One may not be a writer to do so, but one can hire a writing service to get the job done.

As illustrated, there is simply so much to write and yet, few people are writing it all. So, let's get writing.

THE WRITING BUSINESS
COPYRIGHTS:

If you are going to take your writing seriously, then you also need to know about copyrights.

I learned quite late that people can actually steal someone's entire writing work and simply change the name of the author and the ISBN. That was when I had already published some of my works. Sometimes, people just make a few changes in the writing, like changing the headings, rewriting some sentences, and then publish the work as their own. It's also called plagiarism.

The global writing industry has not been without drama regarding this. In 2019, Tochukwu Okafor's story *All Our Lives* was removed from the Cain Prize shortlist for failure to attribute an original source. In 2016, the US first lady, Melania Trump gave a speech at the Republican National Convention that not only mimicked the overall message of Michelle Obama's Speech at the Democratic National Convention, but also used some of the exact wording of her speech. Amazon paperback publication portal has mechanisms to detect plagiarism, but I can't yet rate how reliable it is. However, there are other means you can use to protect your work and they include getting your work copyrighted.

Each country and region has a body that undertakes the implementation of this key aspect on behalf of writers and other publishers. For example, there is WIPO, (World Intellectual Property Organization), IFRRO (International Federation of Reproduction Rights Organizations) and at the national level in Zambia, we have PACRA (Patents and Companies Registration Authority), and more on the private side, we have ZARRSO (Zambia Reprographic Rights Organization). One pays a fee to get their works copyrighted.

The copyright organization tries as much as possible to track every reprint of the author's works and collect proceeds from the same on behalf of the author.

However, the most basic line of protection against plagiarism and reproduction without the consent of the author is usually a copyright page that is inserted in the work's front matter.

JENNIPHER M. ZULU

GOVERNMENT'S ROLE:

Governments play a big role in the writing sectors of many countries. It's the governments that set enabling environments for the establishment and growth of the writing industries through policy formulation and implementation and by setting up deliberate supporting programs and structures for skills development and promotion of both arts, and the sector.

In 2015, I co-founded the Southern Writers Bureau with a writer colleague. Our vision was clear. Our creative writing sector and industry were near nonexistent. Our pursuit was exhilarating because the future we saw was very bright. We were pioneering a journey.

However, when we started and got knocking on different doors for help and support to achieve our dreams, we soon learned that what we embarked on, was nowhere easy to realize. We also soon learned that we needed a lot of support from the government specifically than any other stakeholder.

Through policy, governments can allocate funding for sector support and development, which goes a long way to establish and grow the sector. I once attended a high-level budget consultative workshop with participants from the Ministry of Finance, parliament, the National Arts Council, and the Office of the President. The workshop was enlightening on aspects of the budget process and funding consideration and allocation. I also learnt there is due consideration for the sector when policy is in place and when sector player voices are heard.

Bookstores were charging high percentages for vending services. And, some of them were rejecting local works, saying outrightly, '*we don't accept books by local authors.*' It was outrageous. I wondered where they wanted us to sell our books. We needed the government's intervention.

Local printing costs were, and still are very high, making pegging competitive prices against quality foreign works very difficult. Readers thus prefer foreign books to local books based on price. We need the government's intervention.

Government is well connected locally and internationally. The linkages can help the sector to find markets, source funding, and help in various initiatives and programs. Government can run various literary programmes through policy implementation and engage society at different levels, including running the programmes in schools, learning institutions, and other entities.

To date, it has proved very difficult for us to achieve our goals because of the many existing gaps and the need for the government to fully play its role in developing and growing the sector.

INSPIRATION NOTE:

When I took to write this book, I wanted first for the writers to understand writing as a business in an industry with other fully functioning businesses feeding into it. I have encountered many writers looking for free services, from editing to cover design, formatting, and even printing. It is from this perspective that I wanted writers to understand that people offering these services are not standing out there to offer free services. They are people who are looking to earn an income from these services.

I also thought of many other people who know very little about writing; who think taking writing seriously is a waste of time. I wanted this category to see that there is more to writing and that there are many great opportunities in writing. I also wanted them to see that if this is taken seriously and with the right principles and strategies at play, writing can yield so much more than just the mere benefit of earning royalties for the writer.

The third category of people I had in mind were people who can't write themselves but have something to communicate. People whose published work or stories carry an important message; a necessary message. I wanted these people to know that there are means employable to get that very important message out there.

To everyone, I hope you have thoroughly enjoyed reading this book. I pray this book has inspired you to write or to get your works written. But more than that, I pray that this book has helped you to look at writing as a business and that you will approach it as such. Let's all look at writing as a business and derive the maximum benefits from it.

ABOUT THE AUTHOR

Zambian writer, Jennipher .M. Zulu, is an enthusiast when it comes to issues of writing. She is a founding member of the Southern Writers Bureau, an organization that looks to bring Zambian writers together, so as to influence the establishment and growth of the writing sector in Zambia. She is a holder of a degree in Business Administration, and has certifications in Social work, Project Planning, and Project Management.

Jennipher is an experienced writer and business strategist with a passion for helping aspiring authors turn their writing dreams into successful careers. With a deep understanding of the writing industry and a proven track record in business management, Jennipher M. Zulu offers invaluable insights and practical advice for writers at all stages of their journey.

Whether you're a budding writer looking to publish your first book or an established author seeking to enhance your business acumen, this book will equip you with the knowledge and tools you need to succeed. Writing is more than an art—it's a business. Start your journey to professional writing success today!

Booth W.C., *The Craft of Research, 2nd edition*, Chicago Guides

Briggs L., *The Six-Figure Freelancer: Your Roadmap to Success in the Gig Economy*, 2020, Entrepreneur Press

Maum C., *Before and After the Book Deal: A Writer's Guide to Finishing, Publishing, Promoting, and Surviving Your First Book*, 2020, Catapult

Friedman J., *The Business of Being a Writer (Chicago Guides to Writing, Editing, and Publishing*, 2018

Read 15/07/22 from http://www.caineprize.com/press-releases/2019/9/3/caine-prize-response-to-allegations-against-all-our-lives

Read 15/07/22 from https://examples.yourdictionary.com/what-are-famous-examples-of-plagiarism.html

Read 23/04/2023 from https://www.legalzoom.com/articles/how-to-start-a-writing-business

Read 25/11/2023 from https://joesolari.com/treating-your-writing-like-a-business/